ALPHABETICAL ORDER

How the Alphabet Began

Tiphaine Samoyault

VIKING

VIKING
Published by the Penguin Group
Penguin Putnam Inc., 375 Hudson Street, New York, New York 10014, U.S.A.
Penguin Books Ltd, 27 Wrights Lane, London W8 5TZ, England
Penguin Books Australia Ltd, Ringwood, Victoria, Australia
Penguin Books Canada Ltd, 10 Alcorn Avenue, Toronto, Ontario, Canada M4V 3B2
Penguin Books (N.Z.) Ltd, 182–190 Wairau Road, Auckland 10, New Zealand

Penguin Books Ltd, Registered Offices: Harmondsworth, Middlesex, England

First published in 1996 in France under the title *Le Monde des Alphabets* by Circonflexe
English translation first published in 1998 in the United States of America by Viking, a member of Penguin Putnam Inc.

1 3 5 7 9 10 8 6 4 2

Original French language text by Tiphaine Samoyault
Translated by Kathryn M. Pulver
Design and illustrations by Frida Φodox

LIBRARY OF CONGRESS CATALOG CARD NUMBER: 97-61745
ISBN: 0-670-87808-1

Printed in France
Set in Garamond 3

What Is an Alphabet?

An alphabet is an ordered list of about 20 to 30 letters that are used to write the words in a language. Each letter is a written symbol for one of the basic sounds of the language. The word **alphabet** is a combination of the words **alpha** and **beta,** the first two letters of the Greek alphabet.

Though people all over the world have been writing for more than 5,000 years, the first true alphabets weren't developed until the period between 1700 and 1500 B.C., in areas bordering the eastern shores of the Mediterranean Sea. Why?

Thousands of years ago, people wrote messages by drawing pictures or symbols that represented either things or ideas. But this didn't always work, because there were too many symbols to remember. Eventually, the people living in the areas of Syria and Arabia came up with a system of symbols that represented the *sounds* in their words. When put together and sounded out, the symbols created the sound of a word in the spoken language. Now people only had to remember which sound each symbol represented.

Today, the Roman alphabet (A, B, C, etc.) is used by half the people in the world. An infinite number of words can be formed from its 26 letters.

Hundreds of different alphabets are used throughout the world. But they may not reflect every sound that occurs within the language. For example, in some languages, **intonation**—the change between low and high pitch—affects the meaning of a word, but this may not be represented in the alphabet.

Many languages use similar alphabets, but the same letter may be pronounced differently in different languages. For example, the letter "j" in German is pronounced like the "y" in "yes." In the Russian alphabet, which shares some symbols with the Roman alphabet, "P" is pronounced "r."

A consonant must be combined with a vowel for its sound to be heard.

A Be Ce De
E eF Ge aicH
I Jay Kay eL
eM eN O Pe
Quu aR eS Te
U Ve W (double
U) eX Y Ze

Even within the same language, one letter can have more than one sound. In English, the letter "c" has two basic pronunciations: *soft*, as in "celery," and *hard* as in "cat." Many languages use diacriticals and accents to give a letter another sound. For instance, in Spanish, "ñ" is pronounced "ny."

Spelling conventions also vary from language to language. For example, in Italian "chi" is pronounced "kee" and "ci" is "chee," while in English "chi" would be "chee" and "ci" "see." English spelling is particularly complicated because it uses many silent letters such as the "k" in "knee," the "g" in "gnaw," or the silent "e." And one letter may have many different sounds, depending on how it's used. For example, in the word "partial," the "t" makes a "sh" sound.

Languages developed spelling rules because of the different populations who used them—each with their own sounds and backgrounds. Often the rules were determined by a society's history or geography. Because England was occupied by Celts, Angles, Saxons, Romans, and Normans (French) at various times, English spelling reflects conventions of all these languages.

The Sounds of the English Language

Vowels in English are divided into checked vowels, which must be followed by a consonant, and free vowels, which stand alone. Consonants are divided into categories by how the sound is produced.

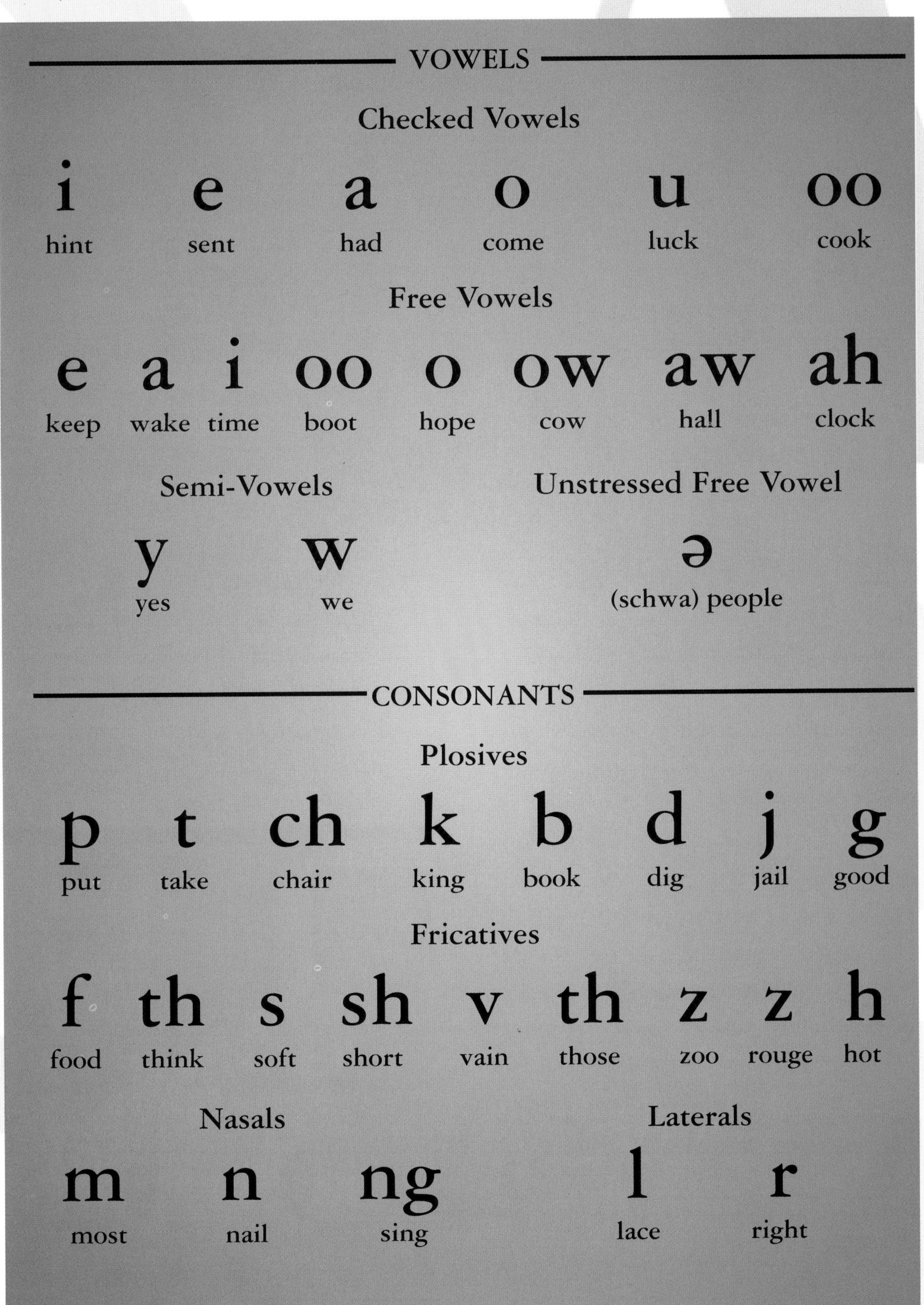

VOWELS
Checked Vowels
i e a o u oo
hint sent had come luck cook
Free Vowels
e a i oo o ow aw ah
keep wake time boot hope cow hall clock
Semi-Vowels
y w
yes we
Unstressed Free Vowel
ə
(schwa) people
CONSONANTS
Plosives
p t ch k b d j g
put take chair king book dig jail good
Fricatives
f th s sh v th z z h
food think soft short vain those zoo rouge hot
Nasals
m n ng
most nail sing
Laterals
l r
lace right

Writing and Alphabets

Why Did People Begin Writing?

Alphabets didn't just appear. The earliest writing started long before alphabets, when people began to connect meaning with natural or manmade markings. We have found forms of writing from as far back as around 3400 B.C. in Mesopotamia and China.

The inscriptions that appear on this ancient clay tablet are in cuneiform, and probably represent the number of animals traded.

In almost every civilization, the earliest writing was connected to religion and magic. Priests were always looking for signs from the gods—literally. They looked on tortoise shells or inside animal livers, and they found them! Perhaps a squiggle or a circle—anything that looked like a distinctive mark—could be seen as a message from a god, which had to be interpreted. Ultimately, these interesting shapes and patterns or "divinations" may have been the inspiration for developing written language. In fact, the name of one early writing system, "hieroglyphics," means "priest-writing." But writing was quickly put to use for financial life and daily activities as well.

Ideograms and pictograms were some of the earliest writing systems. These systems do not use an alphabet: they use pictures and symbols and represent more complicated ideas by combining signs.

The oldest known writing system is called **cuneiform.** It was invented by the Sumerians, who lived in Mesopotamia (part of modern-day Iraq) more than 5,000 years ago.

What were the conditions in Mesopotamia that gave its citizens a need for writing? It is helpful to look at the whole picture. Mesopotamia was a civilization rich in certain raw

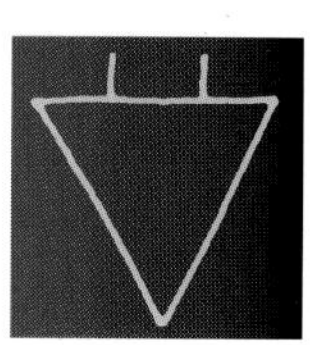
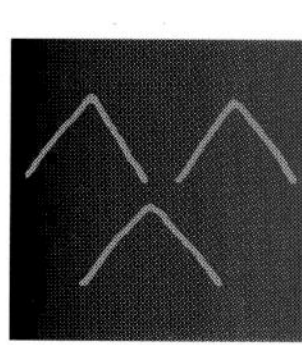
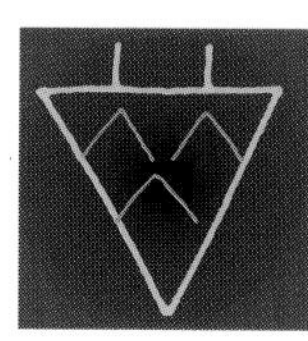

Combining the pictograms that stand for "ox" and "mountain" creates the ideogram that stands for "wild game."

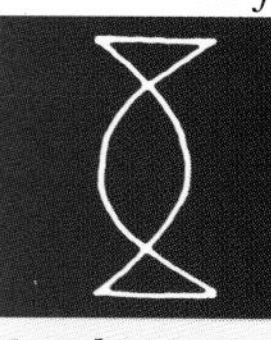
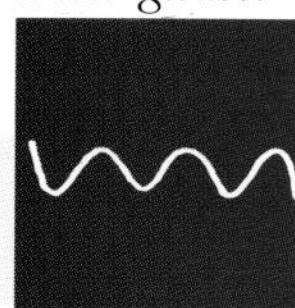
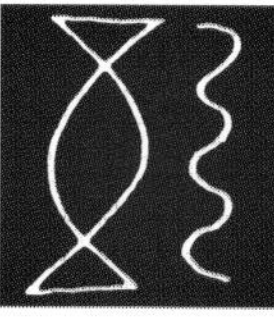

Combining the pictograms that stand for "jug" and "water" creates the ideogram for "fresh."

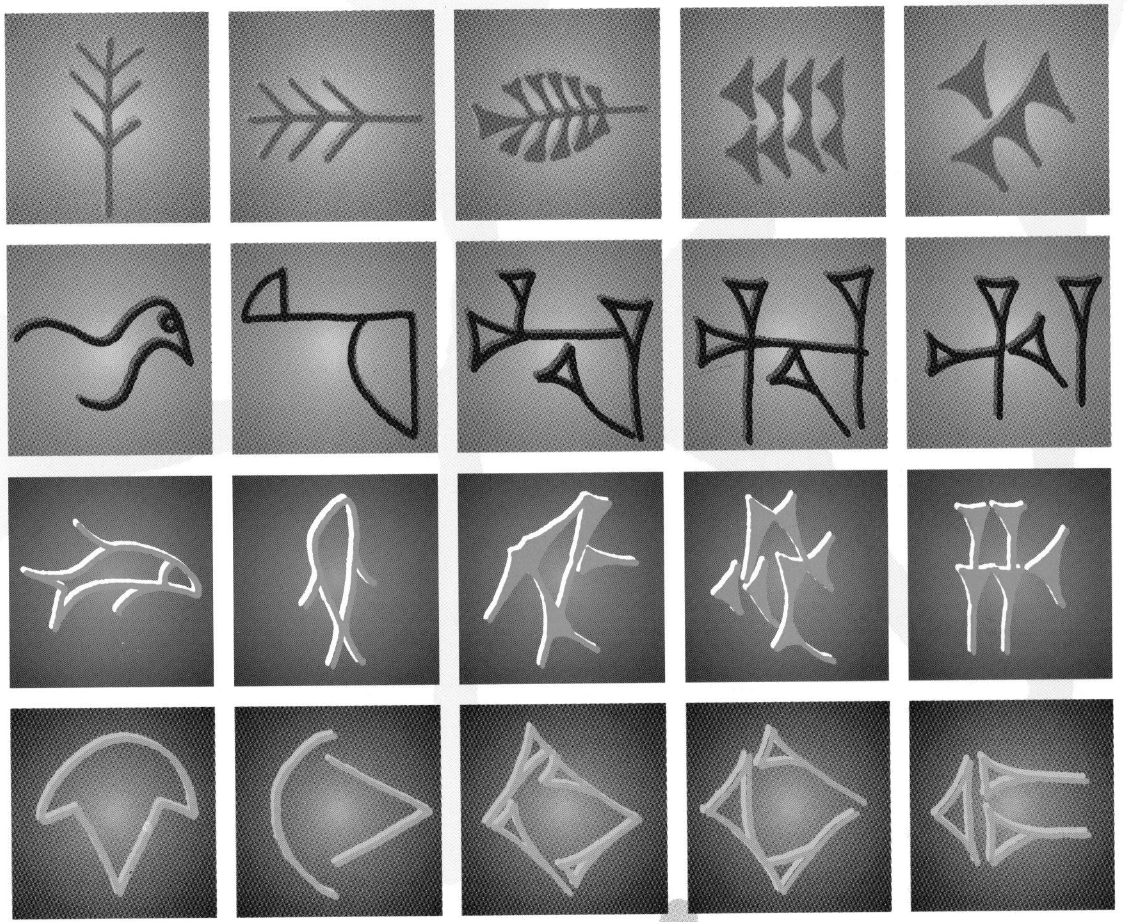

From 3300 to 700 B.C., the cuneiform writing system evolved from pictograms to abstract signs, as shown here with the changing signs for "barley," "bird," "fish," and "cow."

materials. They had plenty of corn, vegetables, meat, leather, and especially clay. But they were almost entirely lacking wood, stone, and metal, which were needed to maintain a successful society. Mesopotamia needed to trade with other cultures, to acquire the things they lacked in exchange for what they had too much of. In order to keep track of what they traded, they started marking symbols for numbers and items in clay tablets, which then hardened. We call the system "cuneiform," meaning "wedge-shaped," because when a stick or reed was pressed into the clay to make the mark, it left a triangular shape.

Cuneiform was not in any particular language. The symbol for an object could be understood by different cultures as whatever their particular word for that object was. From the Sumerians, cuneiform writing spread to Akkadians, Babylonians, and Assyrians, and eventually became the writing system of the entire Middle East.

Hieroglyphs

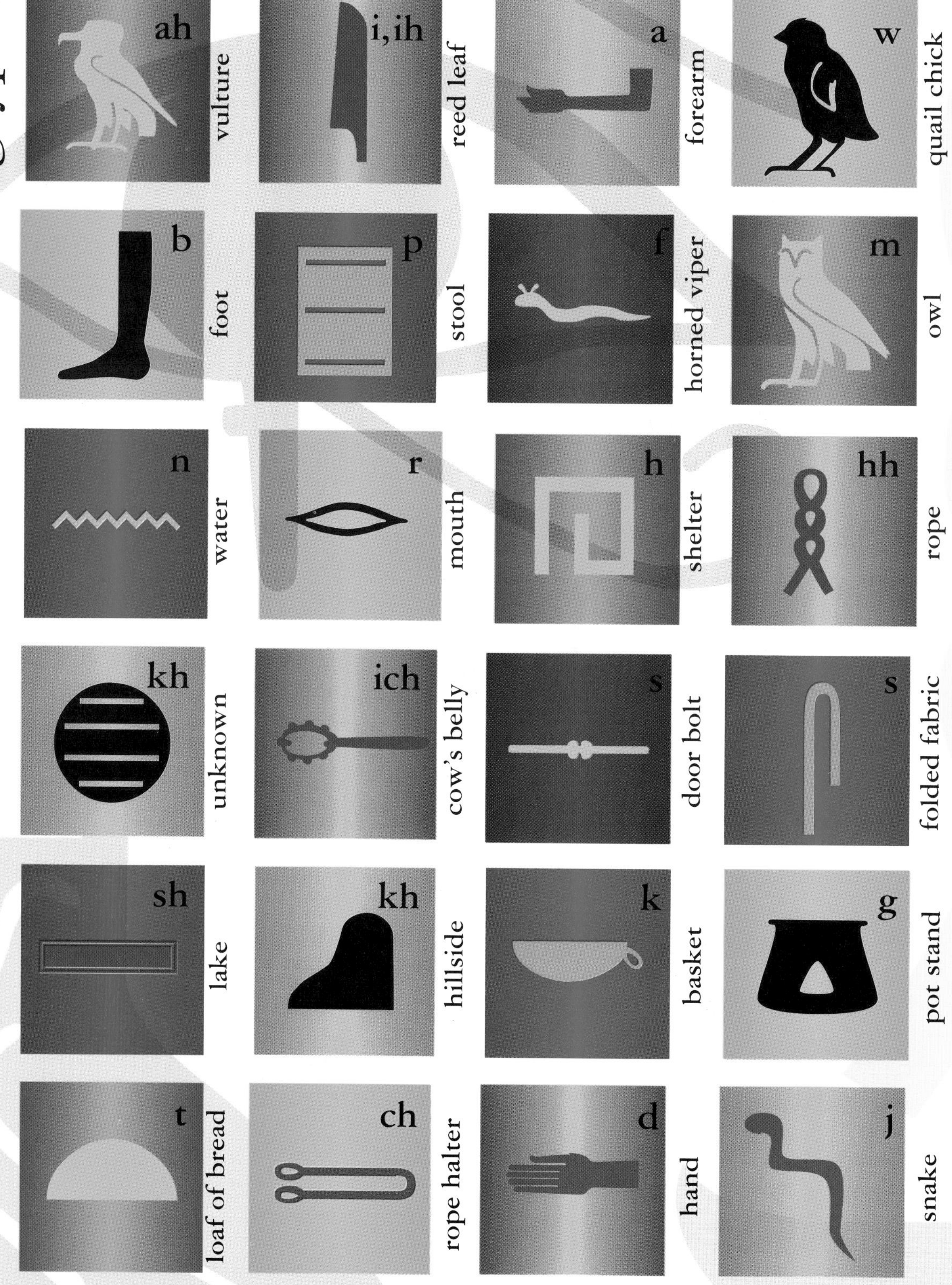

The hieroglyphic writing system includes both pictorial signs and phonetic ones (symbols for sounds). These are some of its phonetic symbols, which can also be used for words.

This hieroglyphic inscription represents Queen Cleopatra. It is entirely phonetic. The "k" and "p" are simplified versions of the forms on the chart.

Hieroglyphics, the writing system used in ancient Egypt, appeared about 3200 B.C., or maybe even earlier. This system was very different from the one used in Mesopotamia—it was a mixture of pictorial signs, which stood for individual things, and sound signs, which represented sounds.

Sound signs, which make up a true alphabet, offer some advantages. Being able to write any word using a small set of alphabetic letters was much more convenient than having a different sign for every single word. Since the letters in a word have no visual connection to the word they represent, phonetic writing is abstract, unlike the concrete pictorial writing. Looking at a word no longer meant seeing a picture and identifying a thing or an idea. Now it meant making connections between symbols and sounds.

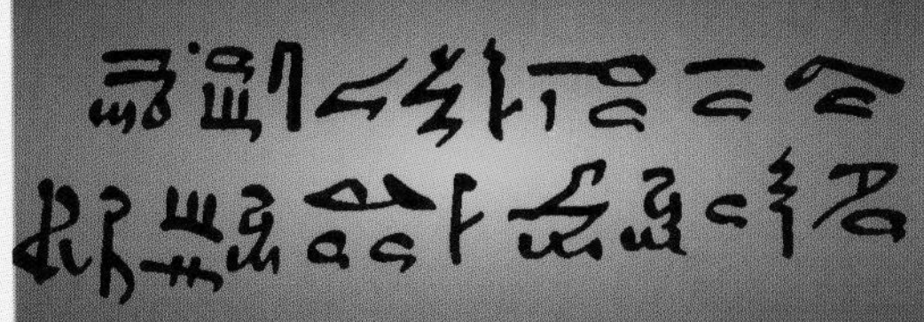

A formula for curing stomach-aches written in hieratic script (above) and in hieroglyphs (below).

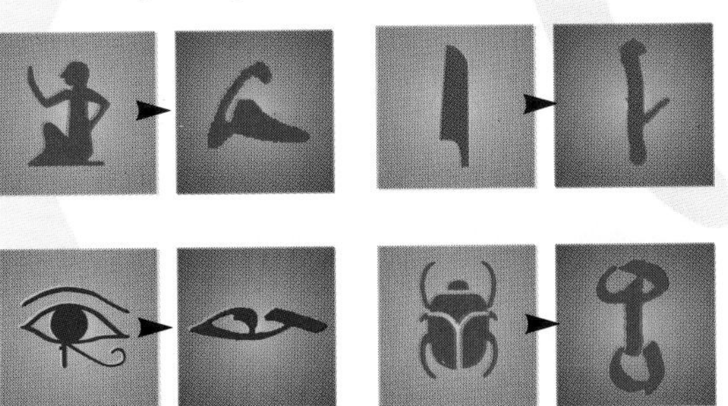

Hieroglyphs slowly evolved into a simpler, stylized form of cursive writing called hieratic.

Woman **Eye**

Man

God

A Family Tree of the World's Alphabets

This is a simplified family tree of alphabets. Linguists have tried to make connections between different alphabets by showing their common origins and where they separated. All our alphabets can be traced back to the same beginnings. Our alphabet, the Roman alphabet, comes from the branch that evolved from Greek to Etruscan and then to Roman capitals. Many other alphabets that are not shown here also branched off from this tree.

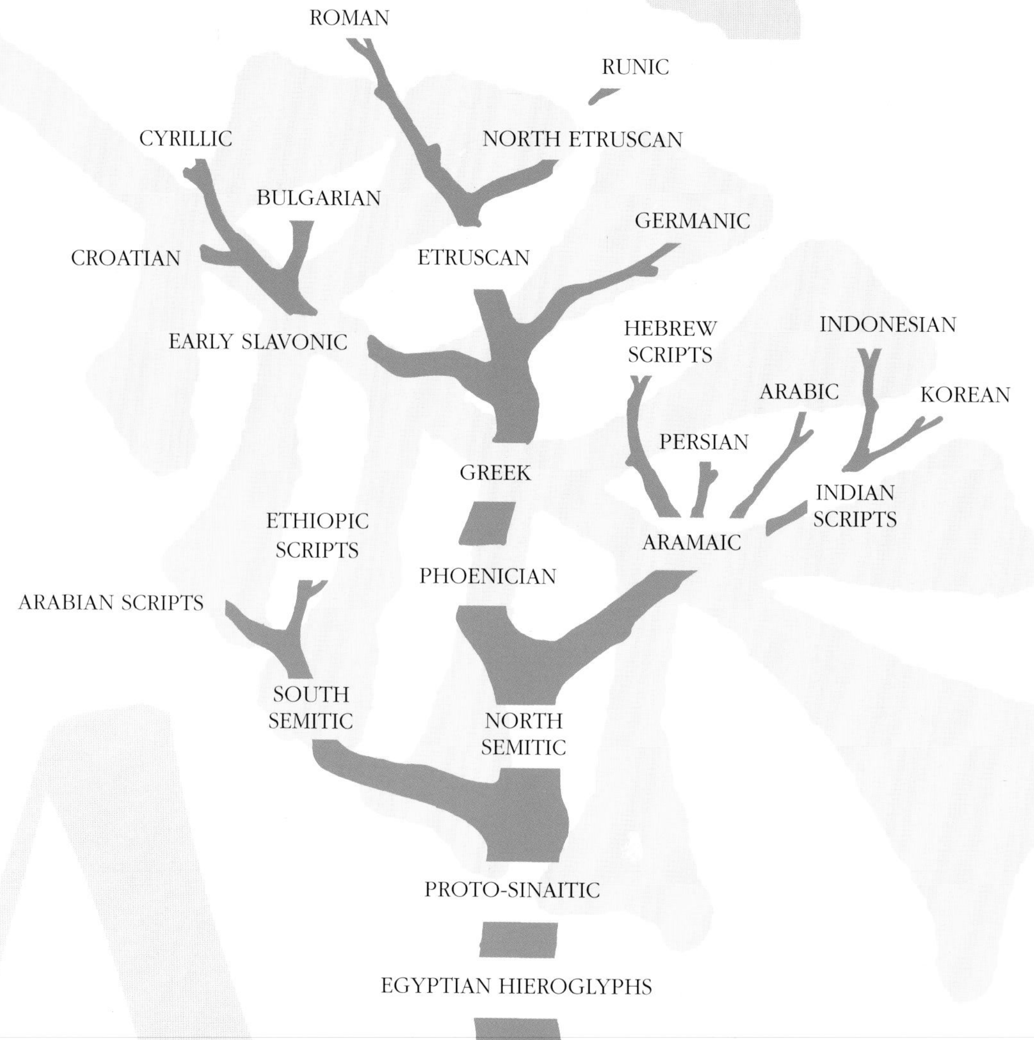

The First Alphabets

The Ugaritic alphabet, which first appeared in Syria around 1500 B.C., was a step up from earlier forms of cuneiform writing. It was a true alphabet, because its symbols stood for sounds in the language instead of entire words. It is named for Ugarit, a large international port where communication was essential and needed to be simple.

Toward the end of the twelfth century B.C., people in Phoenicia (modern-day Lebanon) began to use a 22-letter alphabet. Unlike the Ugaritic alphabet, this one was linear; its letters were made

Ugaritic Cuneiform

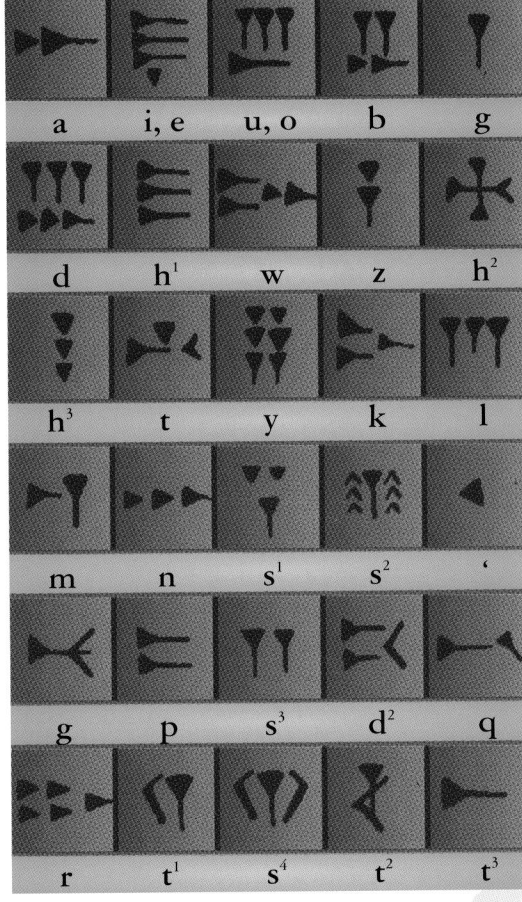

From Egyptian to Phoenician

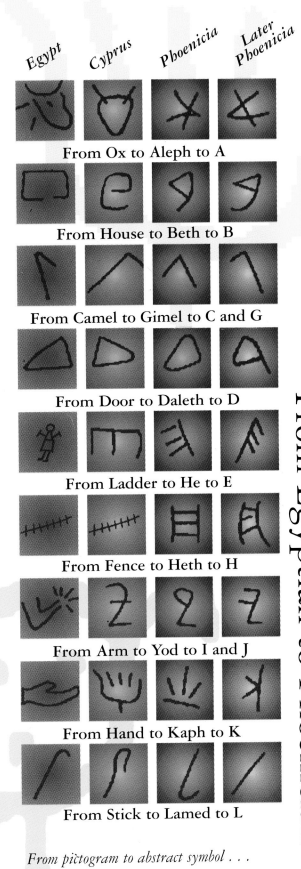

Egypt *Cyprus* *Phoenicia* *Later Phoenicia*

From Ox to Aleph to A

From House to Beth to B

From Camel to Gimel to C and G

From Door to Daleth to D

From Ladder to He to E

From Fence to Heth to H

From Arm to Yod to I and J

From Hand to Kaph to K

From Stick to Lamed to L

From pictogram to abstract symbol . . .

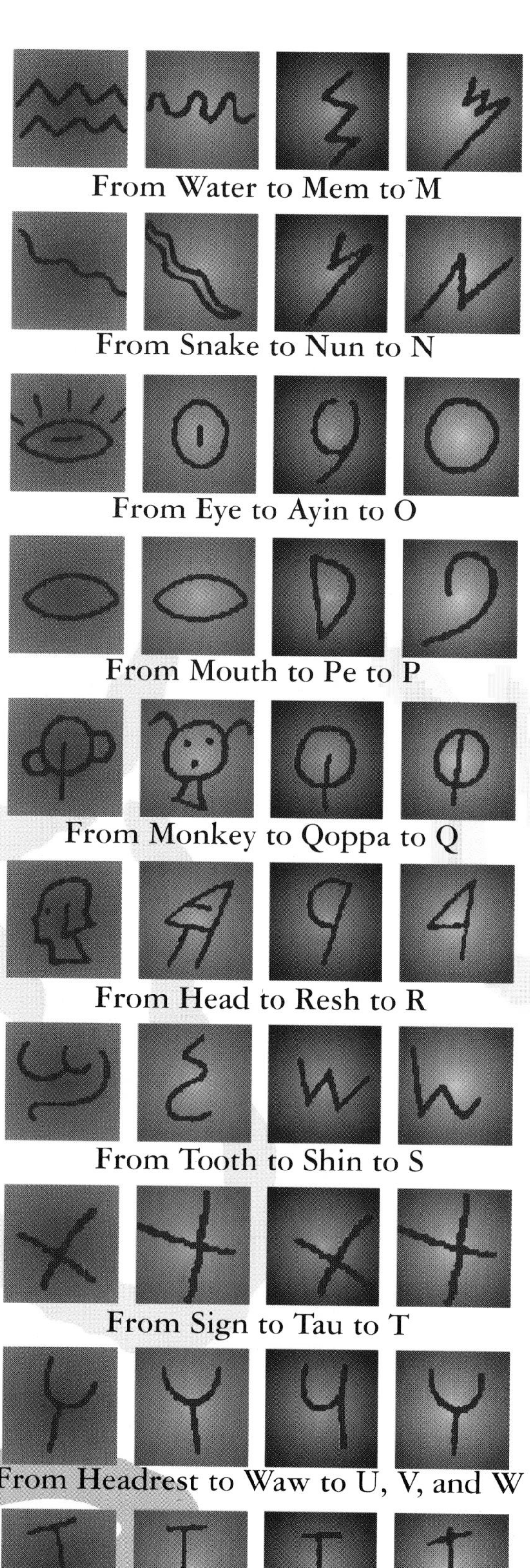
From Water to Mem to M

From Snake to Nun to N

From Eye to Ayin to O

From Mouth to Pe to P

From Monkey to Qoppa to Q

From Head to Resh to R

From Tooth to Shin to S

From Sign to Tau to T

From Headrest to Waw to U, V, and W

From Olive tree to Zayin to Z

of lines instead of triangles. This very significant change took place when different writing materials began being used. On clay tablets, it was hard to do anything but impress simple pictures, but the Phoenicians used papyrus, a smooth paperlike substance from the papyrus plant, with a flat surface more suited to the finer lines of linear writing.

The emergence of the Greek alphabet from the Phoenician one marked a very important stage in the development of the alphabetic writing systems. All western alphabets come from the Greek, including ones that are no longer in use, such as *runes*, which were the earliest German alphabet.

The Greek Alphabet

The earliest alphabets contained only consonant sounds—no vowels. Since

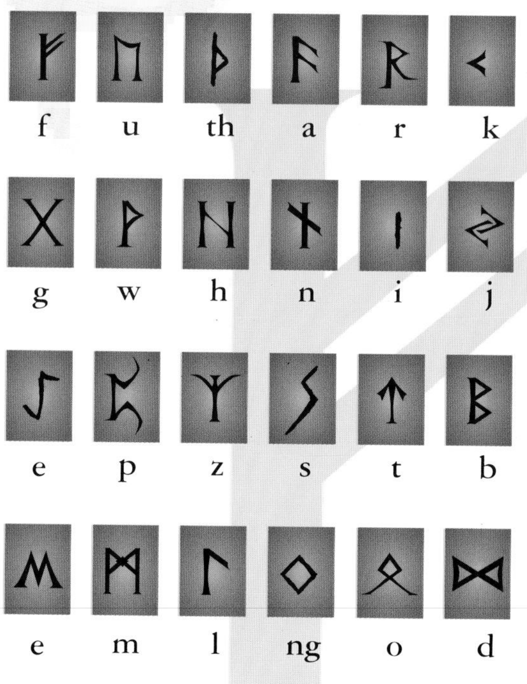

Runes

vowels represent the breathing between sounds, it was usually clear what a word was without them—for instance: "Grk wrtng." But the Greeks wanted to include letters for the vowel sounds, too. They wanted to be able to write down every single sound specifically. They started with the Phoenician alphabet, which had only consonants. Then they took the letters for sounds that didn't exist in Greek and assigned them to vowel sounds instead. They also added letters of their own.

So the Greek alphabet was the first to include all sounds—both vowels and consonants. Syllables, and then words, were formed by combining the letters.

The Etruscan and Latin Alphabets

The Etruscan alphabet was derived from the Greek, and the Latin alphabet from the Greek via the Etruscan. As the Latin alphabet evolved, letters were put to new uses, and new letters were added when new sounds from other cultures needed to be represented. Latin was spread far and wide by the Roman empire and developed into the Romance languages: French, Spanish, Italian, Portuguese, and Romanian. The roots of many English words also come from Latin. The Etruscan alphabet has survived, but we have few Etruscan texts, since the language died out when the culture was absorbed by the Romans.

	Etruscan alphabet from Marsiliana	*Archaic alphabet from Thera*
alpha	𐌀	A A
beta	𐌁	Ր
gamma	𐌂	Γ
delta	𐌃	Δ
epsilon	𐌄	Ε
digamma	𐌅	Ϝ
zeta	𐌆	
eta	𐌇	𐌇
theta	𐌈	⊕
iota	𐌉	ϟ
kappa	𐌊	Κ
lambda	𐌋	Λ
mu	𐌌	Μ
nu	𐌍	Ν
xi	𐌎	Ξ
omicron	𐌏	Ο ⊙
pi	𐌐	Ր
san	𐌑	Μ
koppa	𐌒	Ϙ Ϙ
rho	𐌓	Ρ
sigma	𐌔	Σ
tau	𐌕	Τ
upsilon	𐌖	Υ

The World's Alphabets

The Roman alphabet is the one most widely used today. But many other systems are in use—the Arabic, Hebrew, Greek, Cyrillic, and Indian alphabets, for example. Some of the more ancient writing systems have vanished and been replaced by other alphabets—ones that are simpler or more widely used.

The very first alphabets—Syrian and Phoenician—were made up only of consonants. Today, only two examples of ancient alphabets made up entirely of consonants still exist: Arabic and Hebrew. In these languages, the vowels do not exist within the alphabet. In modern texts, they appear as marks above or below the letters.

All other modern alphabets contain both vowels and consonants. Some of these alphabets are syllabic, meaning that each symbol represents an entire syllable—a consonant and vowel sound together.

There are several different ways to

Arabic

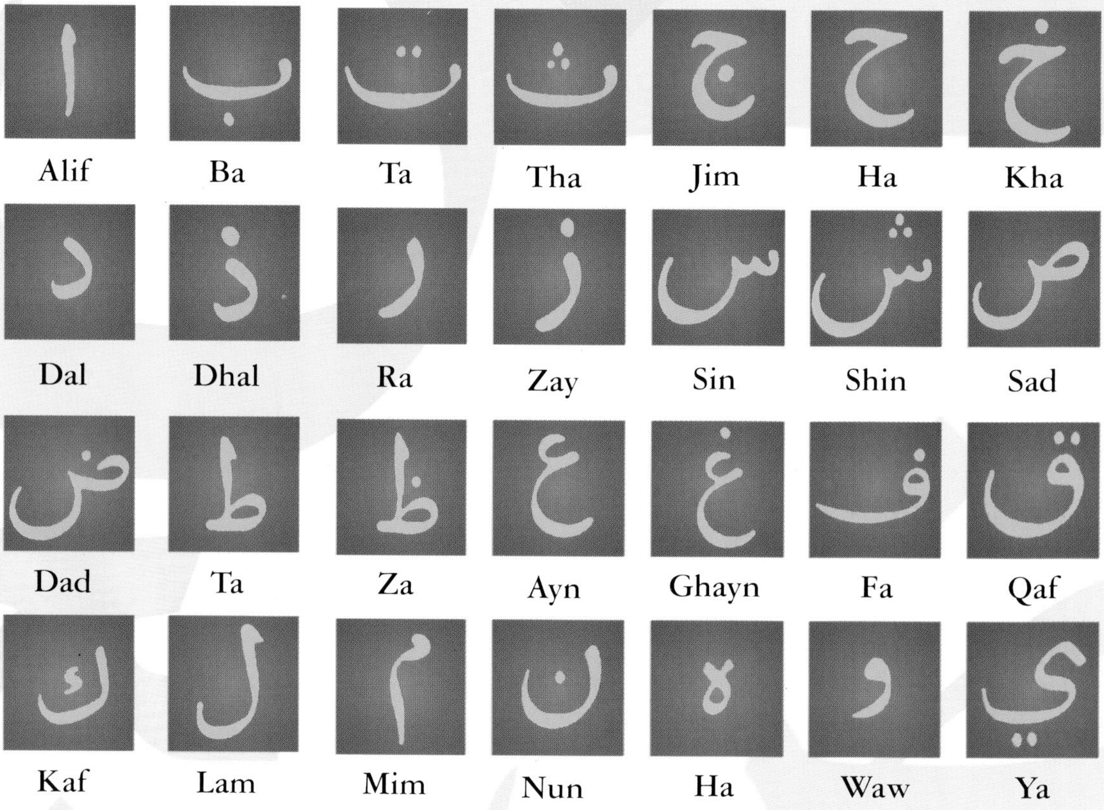

The Arabic alphabet (shown here from left to right), is written from right to left: it has 28 letters and is used throughout almost the entire Islamic world.

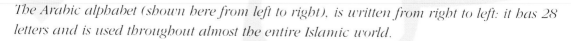

Hebrew

The Hebrew alphabet hasn't changed much since it first appeared. It is also written right to left (although it is shown here left to right).

א	ב	ג	ד
Aleph	Beth	Gimel	Daled

ה	ו	ז	ח	ט	י
He	Vav	Zayin	Het	Tet	Yod
כ	ל	מ	נ	ס	ע
Kaf	Lamed	Mem	Nun	Samekh	Ayin
פ	צ	ק	ר	ש	ת
Pe	Tzadi	Koph	Resh	Shin	Tav

write Japanese. One of these is an alphabet, which is completely syllabic. The Japanese took their original, ideographic writing system from the Chinese in the ninth century. These symbols are known as **katakana**. From them was developed a more flowing form called **hiragana**. When the syllabic form of writing was created, an entire set of syllabic symbols developed in both katakana and hiragana.

The Devanagari alphabet, one of the major alphabets of India, is only partly syllabic, because its characters represent syllables ("ta," "tee") as well as sounds ("t," "p," etc.).

But it was the Greeks who first thought of representing vowels all by themselves in words. The English vowels a, e, i, o, and u correspond to the Greek letters alpha (a), epsilon (short e), eta (long e), iota (i), omicron (o), upsilon (u), and omega (long o). Thus the Greek alphabet was able to represent all sounds, unlike consonant-only alphabets, while using many fewer symbols than syllabic alphabets.

A Japanese Syllabary
Go Ju On

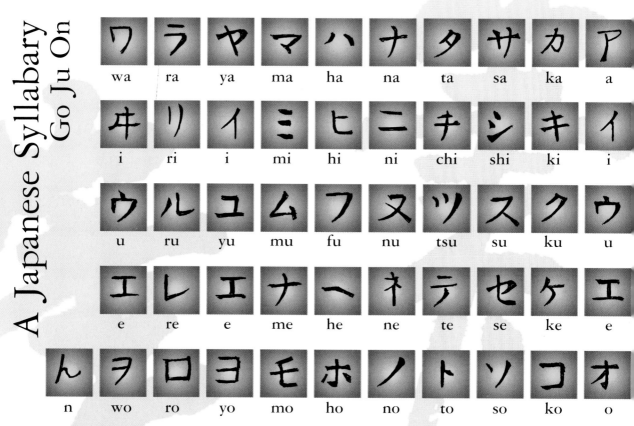

	ワ	ラ	ヤ	マ	ハ	ナ	タ	サ	カ	ア
	wa	ra	ya	ma	ha	na	ta	sa	ka	a
	ヰ	リ	イ	ミ	ヒ	ニ	チ	シ	キ	イ
	i	ri	i	mi	hi	ni	chi	shi	ki	i
	ウ	ル	ユ	ム	フ	ヌ	ツ	ス	ク	ウ
	u	ru	yu	mu	fu	nu	tsu	su	ku	u
	エ	レ	エ	メ	ヘ	ネ	テ	セ	ケ	エ
	e	re	e	me	he	ne	te	se	ke	e
ン	ヲ	ロ	ヨ	モ	ホ	ノ	ト	ソ	コ	オ
n	wo	ro	yo	mo	ho	no	to	so	ko	o

The set of basic syllabic symbols set out in order is called the go ju on. This is the katakana version.

An Indian Alphabet
Devanagari

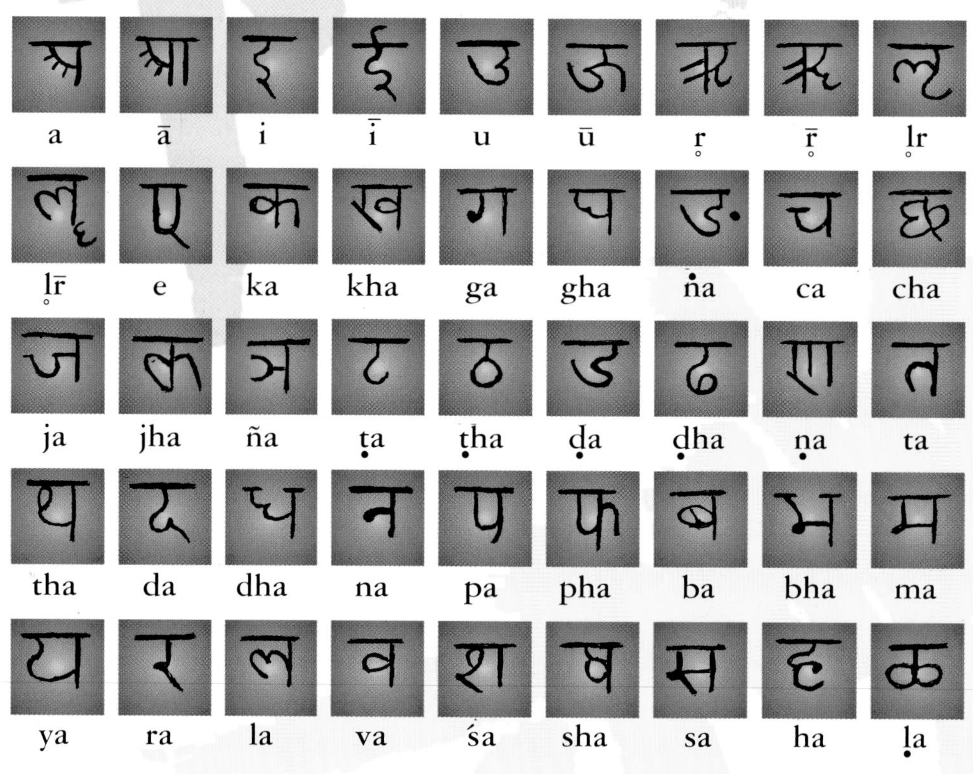

The Greek Alphabet

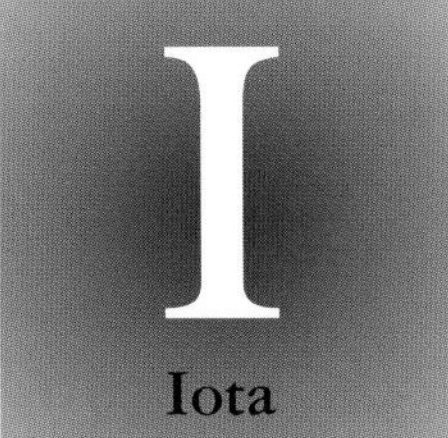

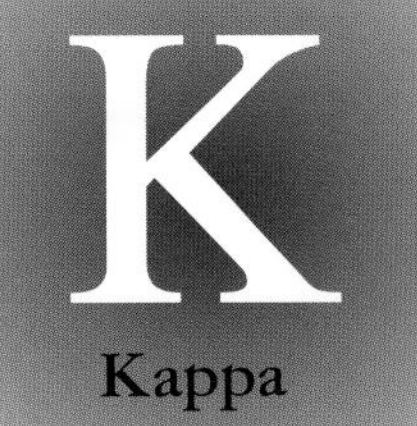

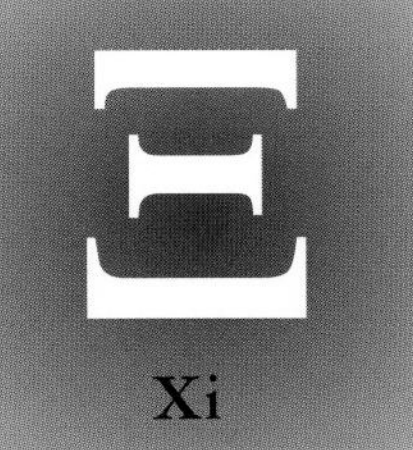

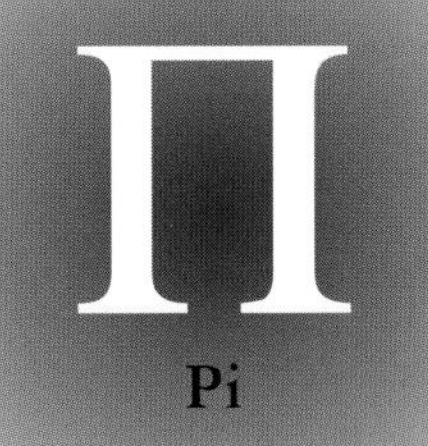

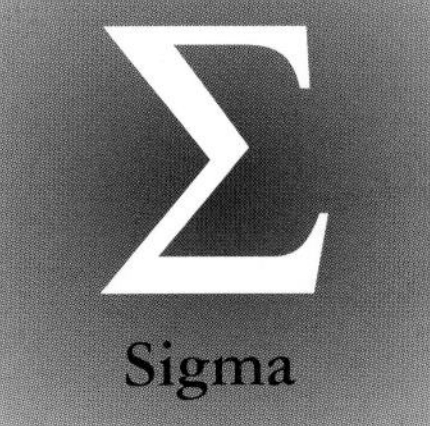

The Latin Alphabet

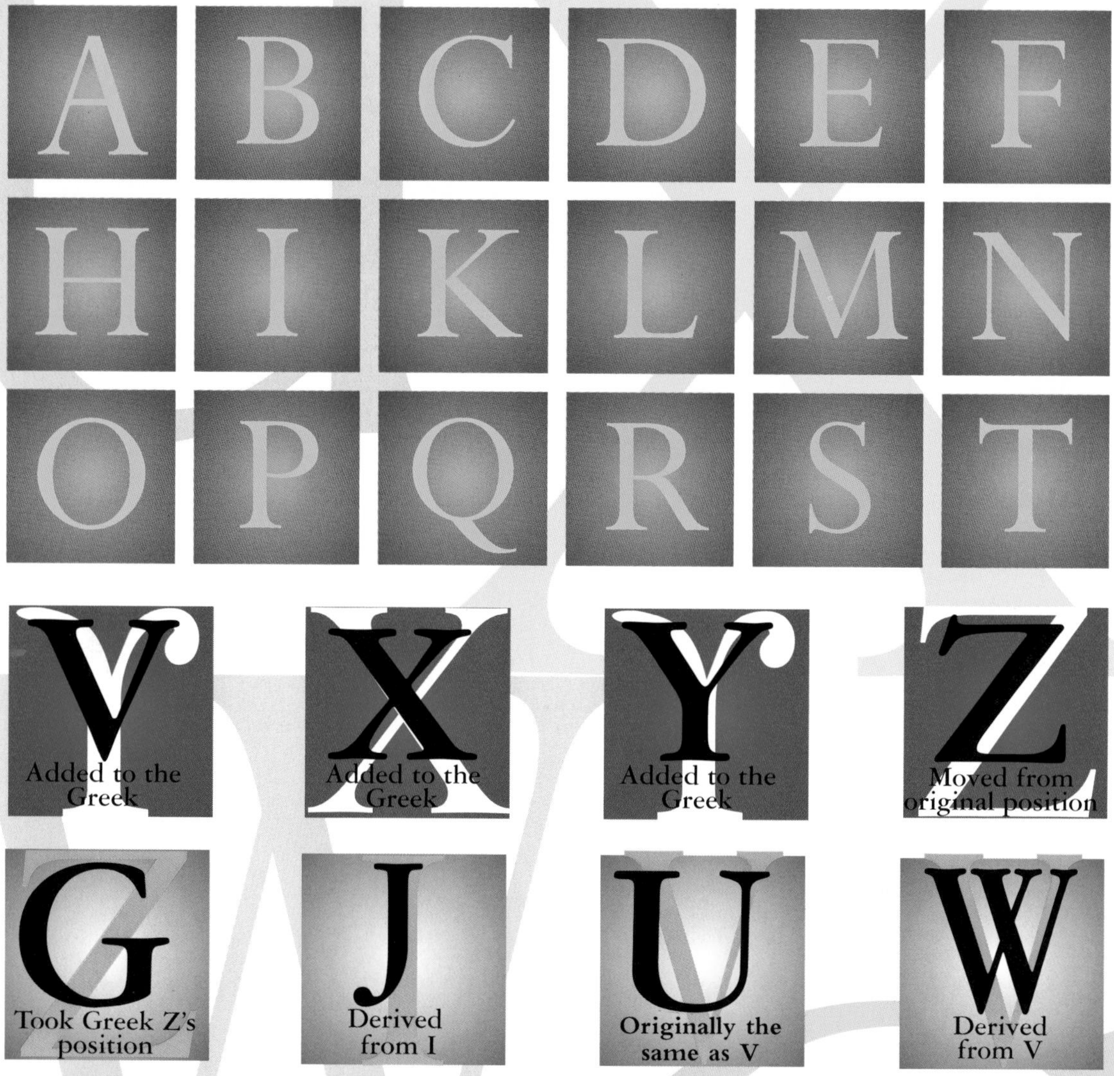

A B C D E F

H I K L M N

O P Q R S T

V — Added to the Greek

X — Added to the Greek

Y — Added to the Greek

Z — Moved from original position

G — Took Greek Z's position

J — Derived from I

U — Originally the same as V

W — Derived from V

The order in which Latin letters appear was based on the Greek alphabet.

The Cyrillic alphabet is another variation of the Greek alphabet. It was invented by a missionary, St. Cyril of Salonica, who converted the Slavs to Christianity in the ninth century. New characters were introduced to represent Slavic sounds that didn't exist in the Greek language. Today, this alphabet is used in Russia, the Ukraine, Serbia, and Bulgaria; however, Poland, the Czech Republic, Slovenia, Slovakia, Croatia, and Bosnia use the Latin alphabet, even though all of them have the same Slav origins.

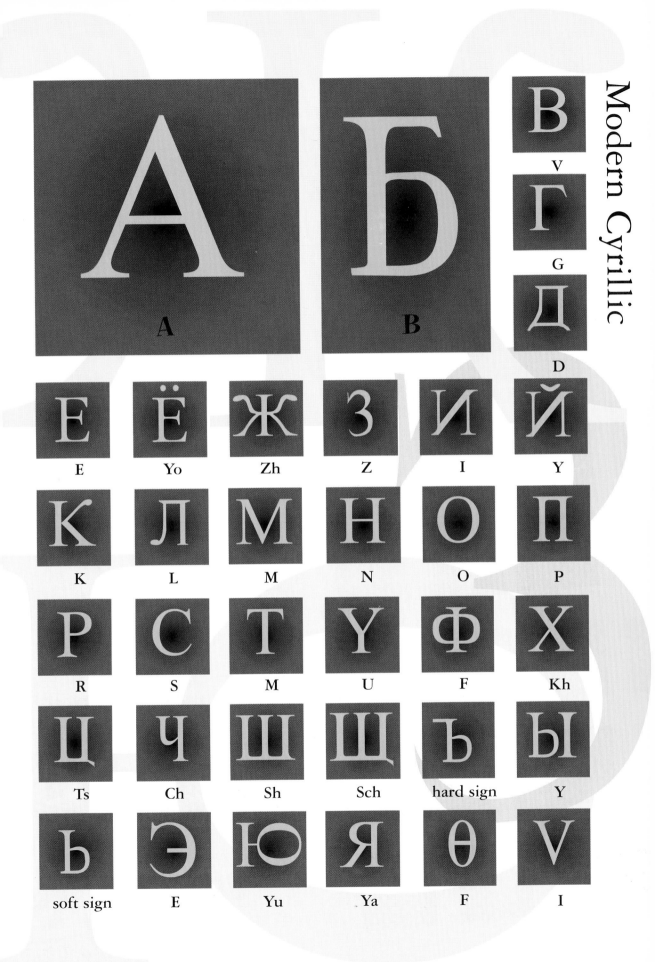

Modern Cyrillic

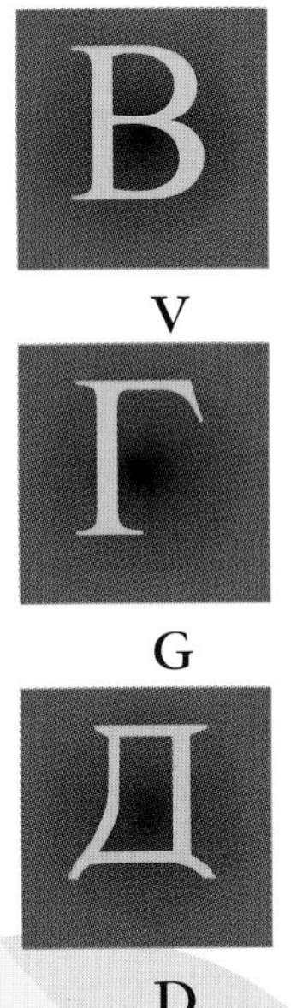

V

G

D

E

Yo

Zh

Z

I

Y

K

L

M

N

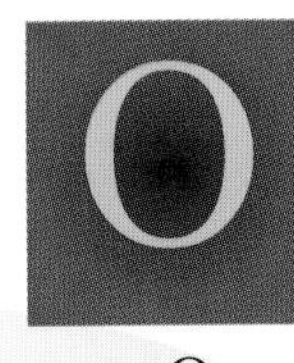

O

P

R

S

M

U

F

Kh

Ts

Ch

Sh

Sch

hard sign

Y

soft sign

E

Yu

Ya

F

I

Calligraphy

Before the printing press was invented, the monasteries and the workshops that copied manuscripts used calligraphy—the art of penmanship or fine handwriting. There are many different calligraphic forms of the alphabet.

A good calligrapher must be very careful to form each character properly. Calligraphy is written using strokes, cross-strokes, and ligatures. A stroke is a broad line produced when the entire nib of the pen is used; cross-strokes are narrower lines drawn with just the edge of the nib; and ligatures are the fine lines that connect the letters. To learn this technique, students had to copy many, many lines of writing, making sure that each letter was exactly the right size.

Over the centuries, the tools and surfaces used for writing have influenced the shapes of letters. Alphabets designed to be carved, such as the Roman capitals, have strong, straight lines. Japanese characters, painted with a brush, have their own characteristic shape. Writing on a smooth surface such as papyrus, vellum or parchment (animal skin), or paper gives more freedom to make curved lines and to write in a continuous flowing line. In the Middle Ages, this freedom gave rise to an alphabet of smaller, more curved letters called **minuscule.** It also led to the art of illumination, in which a manuscript is decorated with elaborate initial letters and miniature paintings, sometimes using real gold.

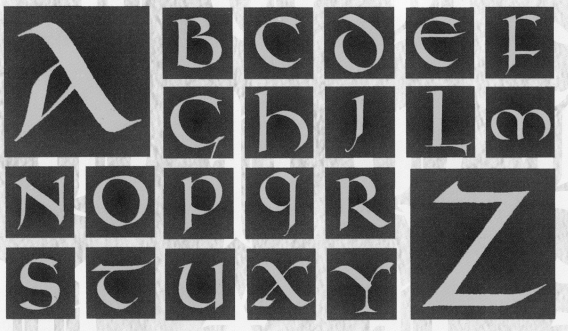

Roman Uncials and Gothic Capitals

The letters above are uncials, a graceful Roman handwritten alphabet used in books starting around the fourth century. When minuscule handwriting become popular, uncials were sometimes used for headings or to start a paragraph, somewhat the way we use capital letters today.

In Northern Europe, manuscripts were usually written in a more angular style called Gothic, which uses straight lines and hooks. Gothic survived in Germany until this century.

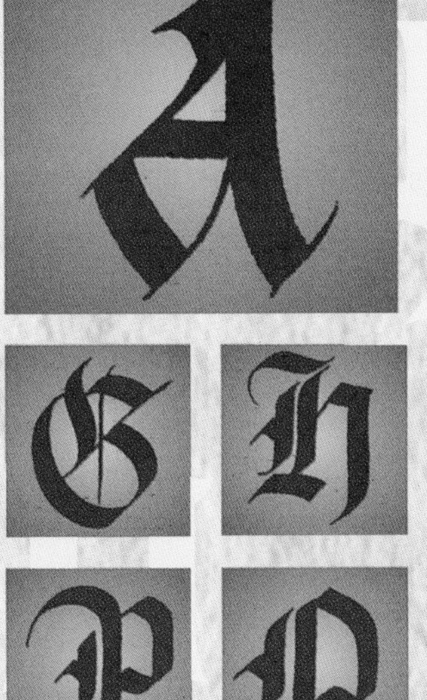

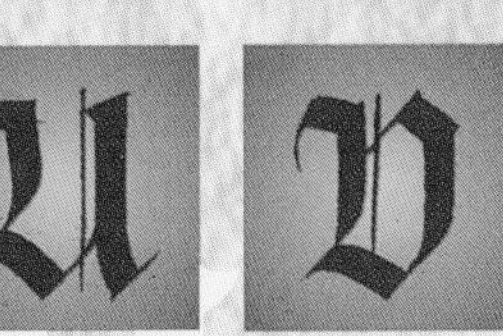

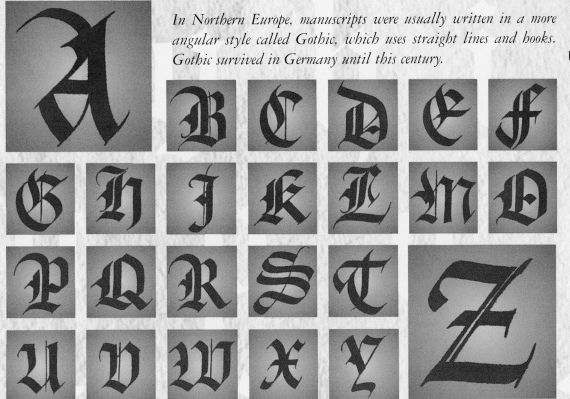

. . . and Typography

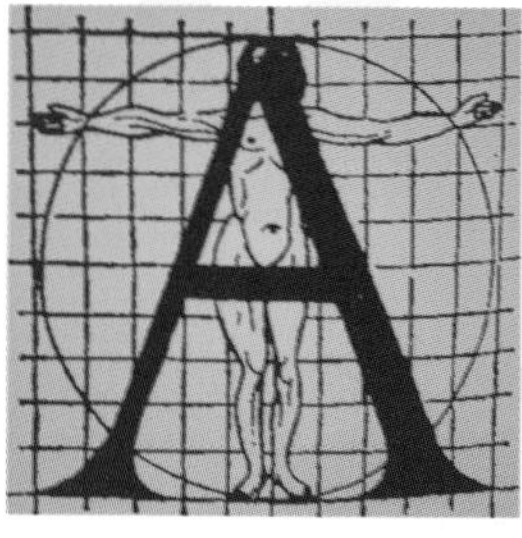

The printing press was invented around 1450 by Johann Gutenberg, using a method called "movable type." He made raised stamps of each letter that could be used over and over again. He was not the first to think of this. The Chinese had experimented with movable type as early as the eleventh century, but abandoned the idea because it was not suitable for their writing system. Since Chinese uses ideograms, with a separate symbol for each word, there were too many different symbols for a printing press to be efficient. Gutenberg succeeded because he had a manageable alphabet to work with.

At first, printers tried to duplicate the work that manuscript copyists had done by hand. Early type was designed to look like handwriting. Capital letters

ABCDEG
HIJKLMN
OPQRTU
VWXYZ
abcdefghijklm-
nopqrstuvwxyz

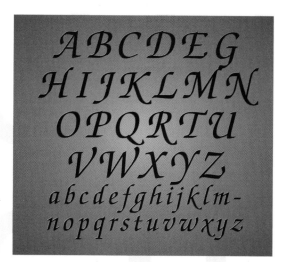

This typeface imitates handwritten calligraphy.

ABCDEFGHIJKLMN
OPQRSTUVWXYZ
abcdefghijklmnopqrstuvwxyz
abcdefghijklmnopqrstuvwxyz

Garamond, a typeface inspired by the letters of the Renaissance, is considered one of the premier typefaces.

A B C D E
F G H I J K
L M N O P Q
R S T U V W
X Y Z
a b c d e f g h i
j k l m n o p q r
s t u v w x y z

This family of letters has extensions at its outermost points called serifs.

were sometimes colored and decorated by hand, with blank spaces left open for hand illumination to be added later.

Mechanical type didn't replace calligraphy at first, but it did compete with it. And it influenced the design and shapes of letters—shapes that had always varied depending on which tools and surfaces were used for writing.

Because many copies of a letter were made from the same mold, the letter would be exactly the same each time it appeared in a printed book, unlike in a handwritten manuscript. Designers worked to create typefaces that would be easy to reproduce, easy to read, and attractive. Many typefaces invented in the Renaissance, such as Garamond and Bembo, are still in use today.

Lowercase letters developed from minuscule writing. Some lowercase letters are very different from their capital forms. Others letters are almost the same in both forms.

The letters below are known as block characters because they're made up of lines whose width doesn't vary.

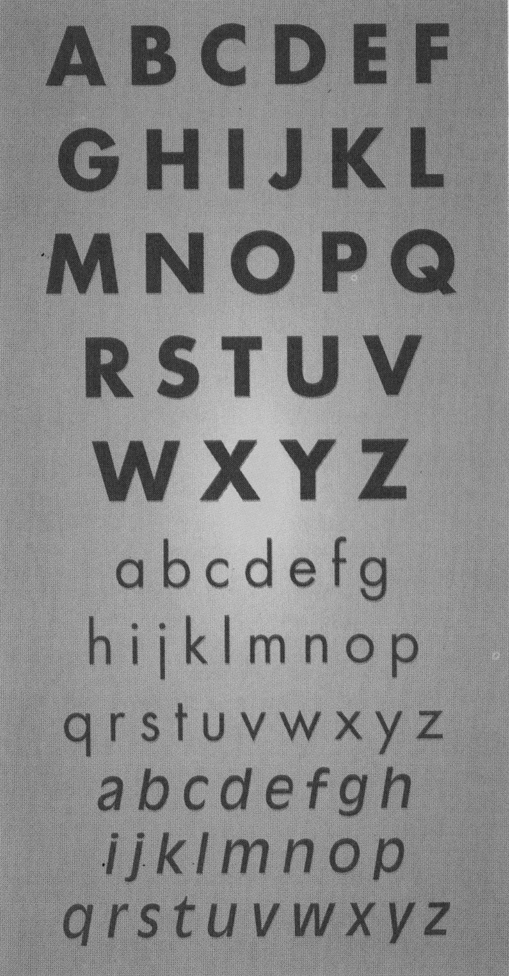

Other Alphabets

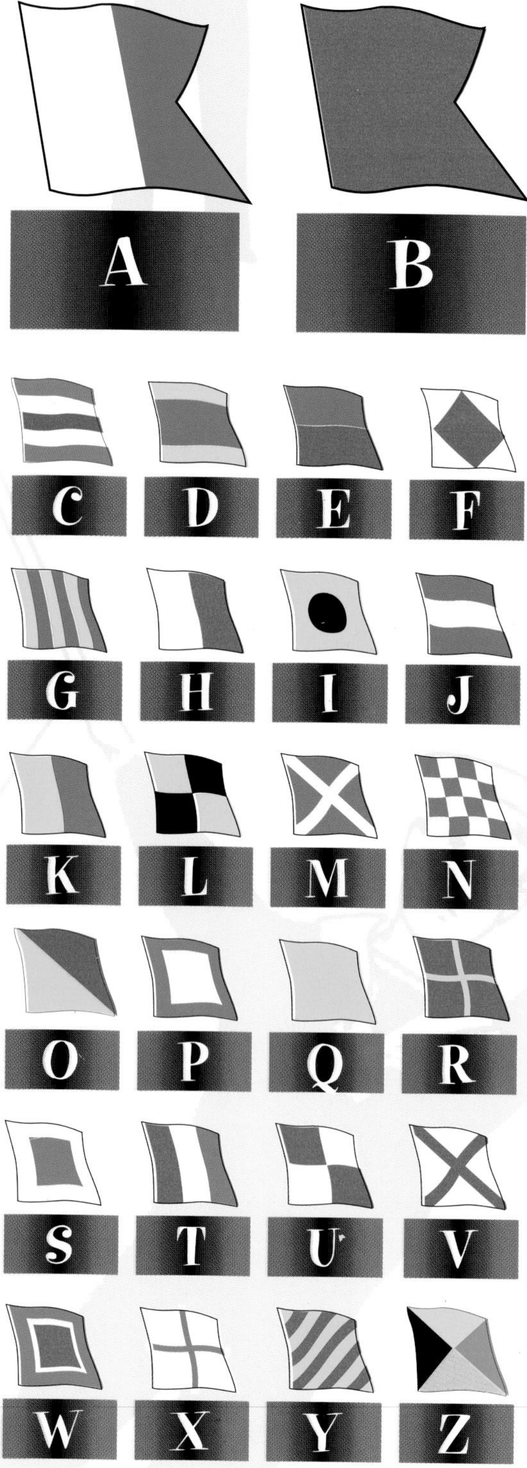

Since people need to be able to communicate under all sorts of circumstances, other symbol systems that could represent the alphabet were invented. Using these, people can form words without speaking or writing—by using lights or flags, for instance.

The semaphore system is often used to allow people on land to communicate with people on boats. Semaphore communication uses two movable arms in various positions. The U.S. Navy signals with the semaphore alphabet, using red and yellow flags. Each movement represents a different letter.

Another international alphabet also uses flags, but in this system, they remain stationary. Each flag has distinctive colors and patterns that can be combined to represent different letters of the Roman alphabet. This "code of the high seas" was devised by the English Navy in the eighteenth century.

The Morse code alphabet uses dots (short) and dashes (long). Each combination of dots and dashes represents a letter or number. Messages can be transmitted by light signals or by an electromagnetic telegraph system that

Semaphores

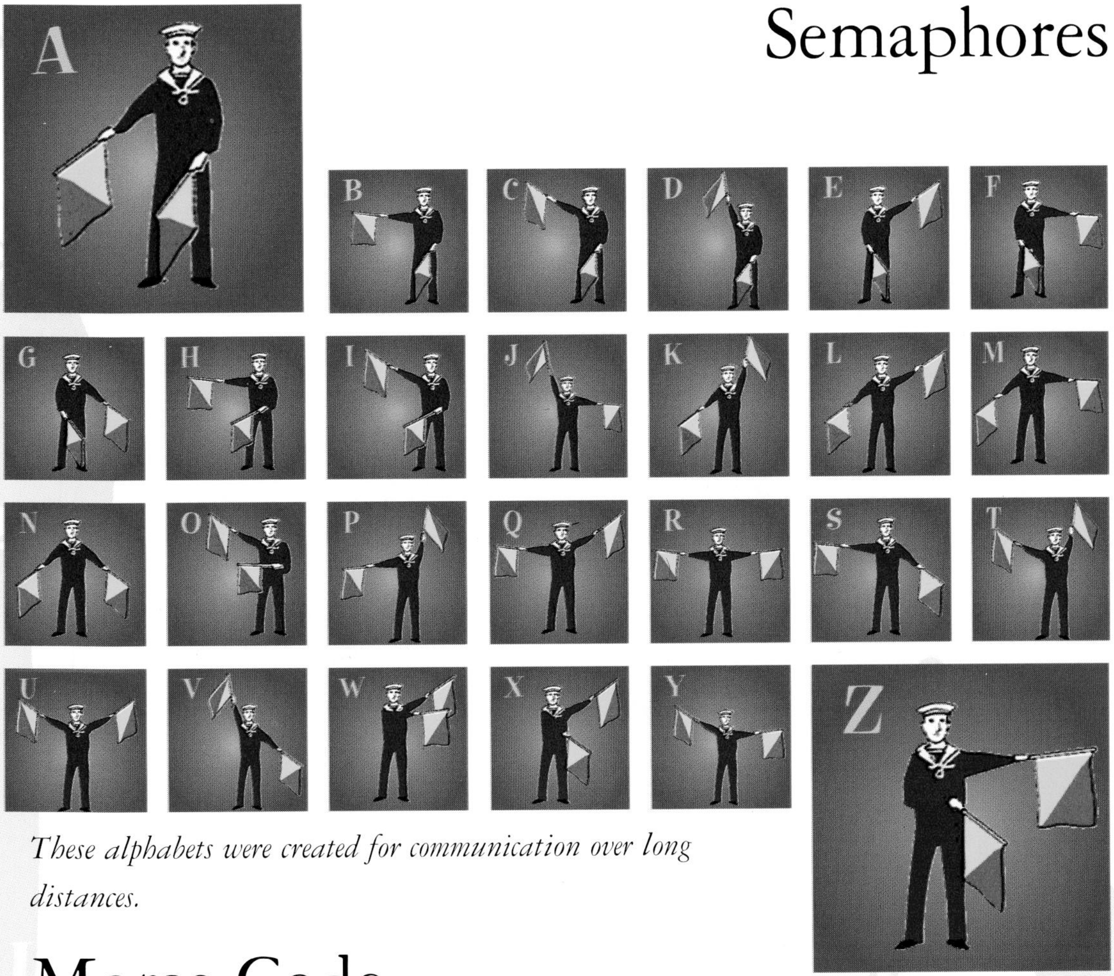

These alphabets were created for communication over long distances.

Morse Code

•—	—•••	—•—•	—••	•	••—•	——•
a	b	c	d	e	f	g
••••	••	•———	—•—	•—••	——	—•
h	i	j	k	l	m	n
———	•——•	——•—	•—•	•••	—	••—
o	p	q	r	s	t	u
•••—	•——	—••—	—•——	——••	•————	••———
v	w	x	y	z	1	2
•••——	••••—	•••••	—••••	——•••	———••	————•
3	4	5	6	7	8	9

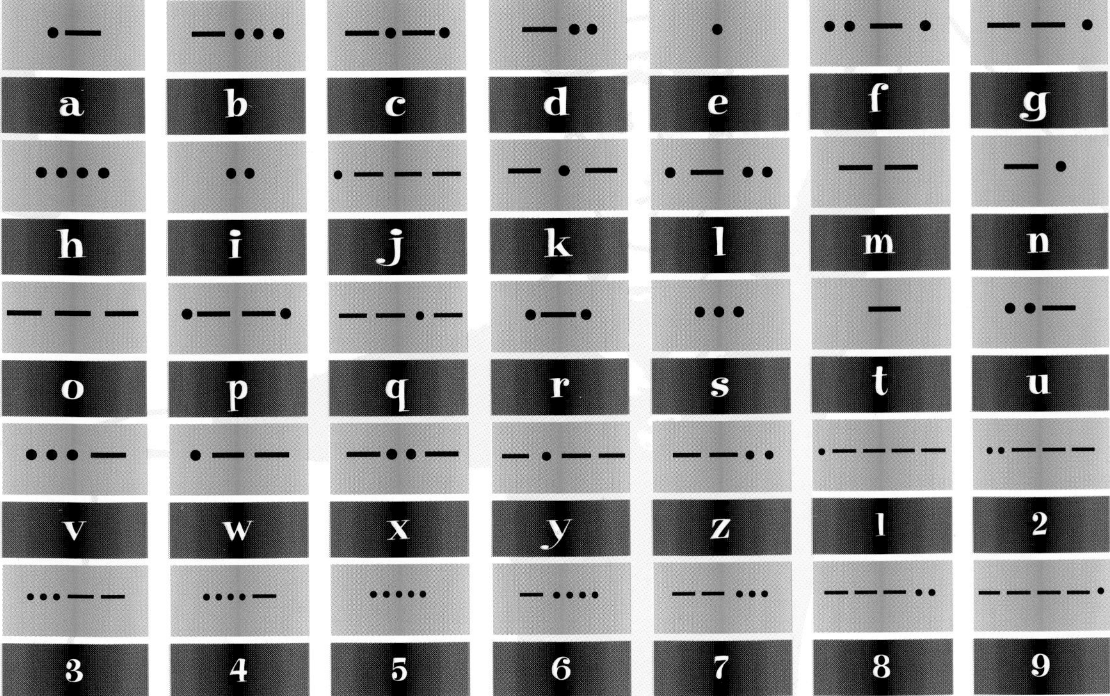

sends clicks. This alphabet was developed by Samuel Morse (1791–1872), who invented the electric telegraph in 1832 and devised this coded system to work with it. The first telegraph line, established in 1844, linked Washington and Baltimore.

People who are deaf often use sign language. The hand gestures usually indicate whole words or ideas, but there is also a hand alphabet where each letter is represented by a hand position. This alphabet is used mostly for spelling out uncommon words or names, not for conversation, because to spell out every word would require too many gestures.

The Braille alphabet is used by blind people. Its characters consist of raised dots, which people can read by touching them with their fingers. Braille is named after its inventor, Louis Braille (1809–52), who went blind at the age of three. He was a professor at the Institute for the Blind in Paris, France, and he devised this system to enable his students to read and write. His alphabet was much needed, and it spread throughout the world.

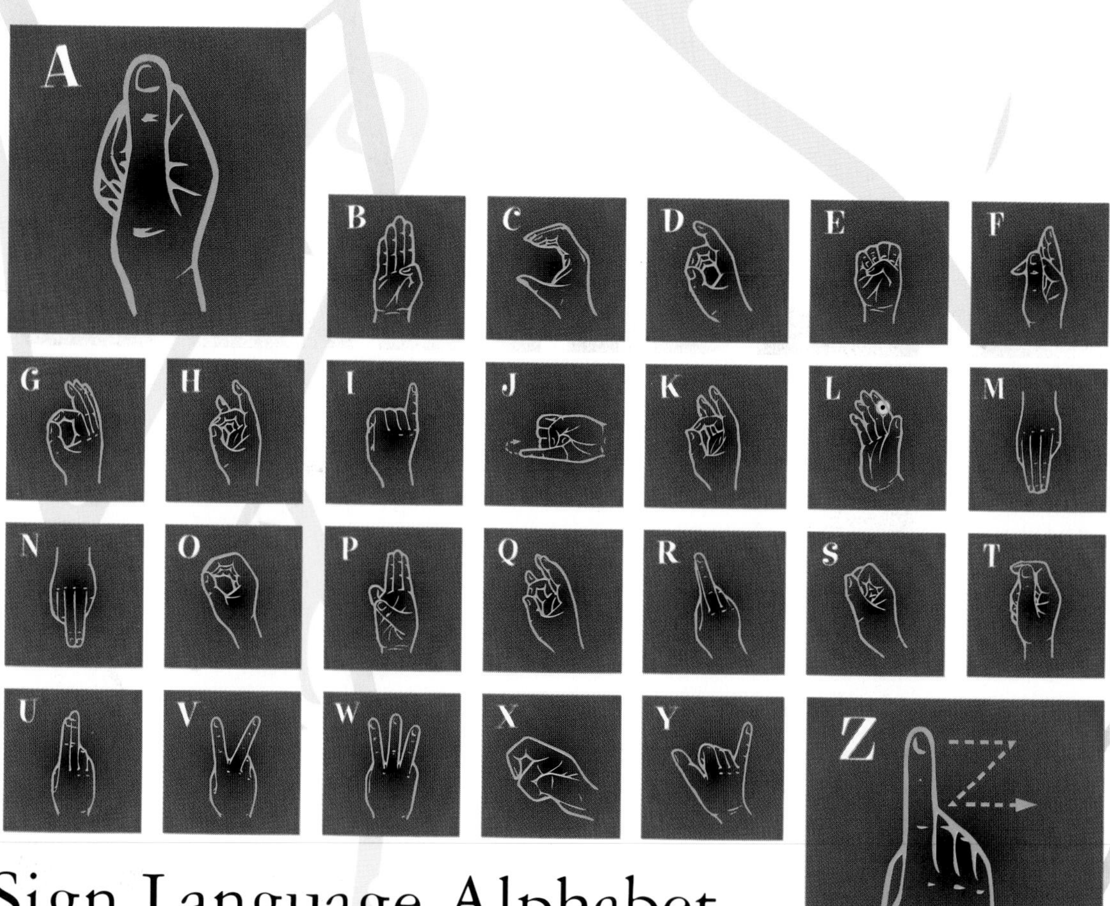

Sign Language Alphabet

The Braille Alphabet

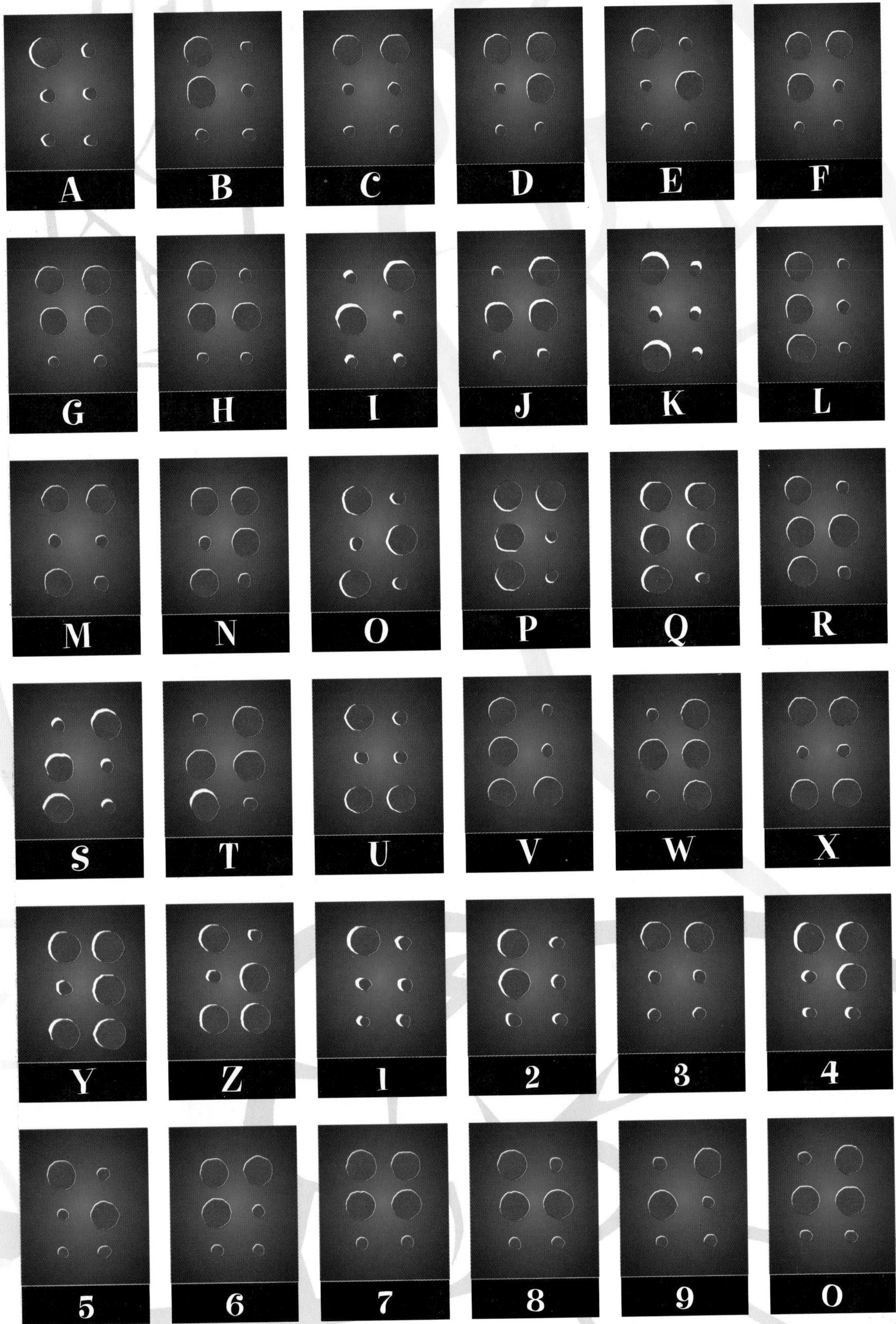

Artists and Alphabets

Chinese writing, like all writing systems based on ideograms, has always been considered an art. Its symbols, which are actually pictures, are often used on decorative artwork. Because alphabets are made up of abstract symbols, they don't lend themselves quite as well to drawing and painting, but they are nonetheless frequently used artistically. Medieval manuscripts often started with a decorative capital letter that had a whole scene painted inside, and later artists have also had fun with the shapes of letters, as in the alphabet below, called "Bizarro."

Artists and writers have thought up interesting and creative ways to use the alphabet. *Concrete poetry* is a cross between art and poetry where words are arranged to visually indicate their meanings. Perhaps the best known example is Lewis Carroll's "Mouse's Tale" from *Alice's Adventures in Wonderland*. What do you see in the other examples?

"Fury said to a
mouse, That he
met in the
house,
'Let us
both go to
law: *I* will
prosecute
you.—Come,
I'll take no
denial; We
must have a
trial: For
really this
morning I've
nothing
to do.'
Said the
mouse to the
cur, 'Such
a trial,
dear Sir,
With
no jury
or judge,
would be
wasting
our
breath.'
'I'll be
judge, I'll
be jury,'
Said
cunning
old Fury:
I'll
try the
whole
cause,
and
condemn
you
to
death.'"

—*Lewis Carroll*

SPIKE SPIKE SPIKE SPIKE
TAIL TAIL TAIL PLATES PLATES PLATES PLATES PLATES PLATES PLATES
AND A TINY LITTLE HEAD
THE STEGOSAURUS HAD SPIKES
SHORT HIND LEGS
SHORT FRONT LEGS

SCALE SCALES SCALE SCALE SCALES SCALES
BE CAREFUL OF THE CROCODILE EYES SMILE TEETH
ESPECIALLY WHEN YOU SEE HIM SMILE TEETH
LEG LEG

—*Janet B. Pascal*

Artists continue to use alphabets in fresh and creative ways—whether by designing their own alphabets or using letters in offbeat new arrangements.

Many authors and poets have written about the alphabet. They've tried to figure out its origins and also give it new kinds of meanings.

Here is a short excerpt from Rudyard Kipling's "How the Alphabet Was Made" from the *Just So Stories.* In this scene, the little girl Taffy invents one of the letters of the alphabet.

"Daddy, I've thinked of a secret surprise. You make a noise—any sort of noise."

"Ah!" said Tegumai. "Will that do to begin with?"

"Yes," said Taffy. "You just look like a carp-fish with its mouth open. Say it again, please."

"Ah! ah! ah!" said her Daddy. "Don't be rude, my daughter."

"I'm not meaning rude, really and truly," said Taffy "It's part of my secret-surprise-think. *Do* say *ah*, Daddy, and keep your mouth open at the end, and lend me that tooth. I'm going to draw a carp-fish's mouth wide-open."

"What for?" said her Daddy.

"Don't you see?" said Taffy, scratching away on the bark. "That will be our little secret s'prise. When I draw a carp-fish with his mouth open in the smoke at the back of our Cave—if Mummy doesn't mind—it will remind you of that ah-noise. Then we can play that it was me jumped out of the dark and s'prised you with that noise—same as I did in the beaver-swamp last winter."

"Really?" said her Daddy, in the voice that grown-ups use when they are truly attending. "Go on, Taffy."

"Oh bother!" she said. "I can't draw all of a carp-fish, but I can draw something that means a carp-fish's mouth. Don't you know how they stand on their heads rooting in the mud? Well, here's a pretence carp-fish (we can play that the rest of him is drawn). Here's just his mouth, and that means *ah*." And she drew this. (1)

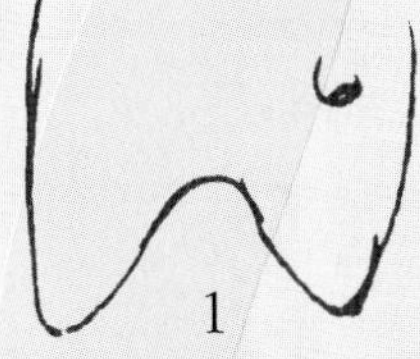
1

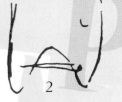

"That's not bad," said Tegugamai, and scratched on his own piece of bark for himself; "but you've forgotten the feeler that hangs across his mouth."

"But I can't draw, Daddy."

"You needn't draw anything of him except just the opening of his mouth and the feeler across. Then we'll know he's a carp fish, 'cause the perches and trouts haven't got feelers. Look here, Taffy." And he drew this. (2)

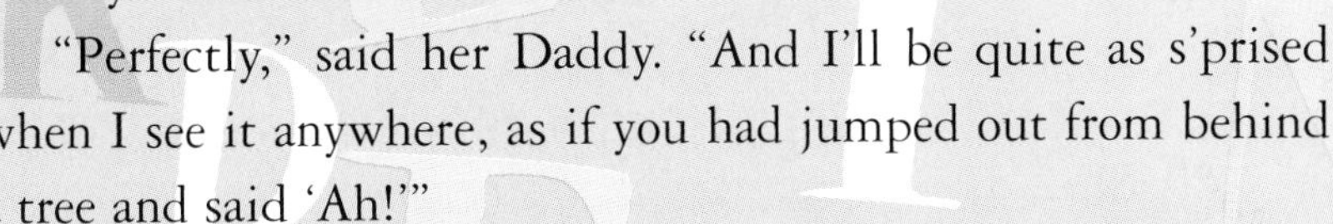
2

"Now I'll copy it," said Taffy. "Will you understand *this* when you see it?" And she drew this. (3)

3

"Perfectly," said her Daddy. "And I'll be quite as s'prised when I see it anywhere, as if you had jumped out from behind a tree and said 'Ah!'"

Glossary

ALPHABET—an ordered list of about 20 to 30 letters that are used to write the words of a language

CALLIGRAPHY—the art of writing beautiful letters

CONSONANTS—the letters of the alphabet that are vocalized with the tongue, lips, or the back of the throat, or any combination of these three

CUNEIFORM—the oldest known form of writing, first used in Mesopotamia, in which a stylus was pressed into a wet clay tablet to leave wedge-shaped marks

HIEROGLYPHICS—the writing system used in ancient Egypt, beginning in about 3200 B.C., which was a mixture of pictorial signs, which stand for individual things, and phonetic signs, which represent sounds

IDEOGRAM—a sign or picture, such as those used in Chinese writing, that represents an idea

INTONATION—the changes between low and high pitch in a word or phrase

LETTER—a graphic sign that represents a sound or small group of related sounds in a language

MINUSCULE—a form of handwriting using smaller more curvy letters than earlier styles

SEMAPHORE—a form of communication using two movable arms in various positions that allows long-distance communication

SYLLABARY—an alphabet, such as various Indian or Japanese ones, where letters of the alphabet represent sound combinations—syllables—instead of singular sounds

VOWELS—letters of the alphabet that represent the breathing between sounds

D.C. PUBLIC LIBRARY
3 1172 04372 7395
LAR.
JUV.
Juv
4/11
SAM
6/99
BAKER & TAYLOR